421903

D0832961

WITHDRAWN
FROM STOCK

designstudio|PRESS

LUMINAIR

techniques of digital painting from life BY NICK PUGH

Dedication

This book is dedicated to my 3 favorite ladies:
my mom Joanne, my wife Eileen and my daughter Serena.

www.nickpugh.com

Copyright © 2006
by Design Studio Press
All rights reserved.

All illustrations in this book are
copyright © 2006 by Nick Pugh

No part of this book may be reproduced or transmitted in
any form or by any means, electronic or mechanical,
including photocopying, xerography, and videography
recording without written permission from the publisher,
Design Studio Press.

Art Direction: Nick Pugh
Graphic Design Consultant: Jane Ward
Design & Layout Production: Marsha Stevenson
Photos by: Eileen Jensen Pugh
Text Editor: Kevin Brown, Joanne Wilkens

Published by Design Studio Press
8577 Higuera Street
Culver City, CA 90232
Web site: www.designstudiopress.com
E-mail: info@designstudiopress.com

10 9 8 7 6 5 4 3 2 1

Printed in China
First printing, December 2006
ISBN-10 1-933492-24-4
ISBN-13 978-1-933492-24-7
Library of Congress Control Number: 2006931914

CONTENTS

foreword

"Where the spirit does not work with the hand, there is no art."
- Leonardo Da Vinci (1452-1519)

An artist—a true artist—works without an art director. Daily, he drives himself to make art. He is his own creative force. Nick Pugh is such an artist, compelled by fascination, observation, and the desire to create.

I have been witness to his talent. One sunny day last fall, I was due to meet him for a working lunch in Pasadena. I was running late. Upon my arrival, Nick presented me with what he called a digital Plein Air painting: a painting of the view from our restaurant table, of palm trees and the beautiful San Gabriel Mountains. This was the very first time I had seen one of his spontaneous works in this vital new format.

Whether they are visions of tomorrow, woven within the eternal present of sunny California, or city scenes of New York, Nick's images depict an America where the future is made every day, often against a background of astounding natural beauty. They also create and hold forth the hidden moment, which if not recorded would be lost from memory. Perhaps this duality is what allows the creation of great art and ideas to rise? The technology has given us all the freedom to create anything we want. And alongside this—innovation, the eternal link to California's legacy of Plein Air painting—speaks softly to our inner soul.

The digital Plein Air paintings of Nick Pugh are no small feat. They are a modern counterpart to the artist's sketchbook. These new works follow in the footsteps of California's pioneer artists who served as illuminators of the Golden State. They produced paintings that told the story of the beauty of California, in a style that often romanticized it. Why? Because the paintings that live on, are more than a depiction of a place. They are paintings that tell the story of how it felt to live and work in California, in the farthest reaches of the western United States, a place where dreams come true.

Ann Field
Department Chair of Illustration
Art Center College of Design

INTRODUCTION

From the earliest cave paintings to the latest in hi-tech photography, artists have sought to capture what they see in representative form. Some artworks are highly stylized and refined; others are more spontaneous and embody the artist's impression of the moment. Many represent the artist's interpretation of the surrounding environment. Art has always involved the use of tools. Over the millennia, new tools, techniques, and media have evolved, but the basic idea of capturing a moment in time has remained unchanged.

The end of the 20th century saw radical changes brought about by the advent of personal computers. One such change has been the use of digital media to create a multitude of new art forms. The addition of new digital tools to the artist's studio has been liberating. High-speed and highly portable laptop computers together with advanced painting software, such as Adobe Photoshop and Corel Painter, make it possible for artists easily to go out into the field and render what they see. The resulting artworks are sometimes called "digital plein air" or "digital life" paintings, but here I will call them "Luminair." Luminair painting is in its infancy, and it is only just being explored by a new generation of creative people.

Several factors joined together to help me develop the artworks presented here. About seven years ago, I was using a home computer to create concept art for the entertainment industry. I also regularly kept a handwritten sketchbook where I experimented with new ideas, forms, and materials. Then, with the purchase of a new Mac laptop, I discovered that my "studio" was portable. All at once, things came together. My sketchbook could be digital, and I could create a stronger, richer visual diary than ever before. And I could do it whenever, wherever, and as quickly as I liked.

Luminair painting is all about capturing a certain light and image at a specific moment in time. The paintings are done quickly on site, and are rarely refined or reworked later. My goal is to give the viewer a glimpse of the place or subject I saw when making the picture in an honest and spontaneous light. There is little or no photography involved, no previously taken image from which to sample color or to manipulate forms. I find this technique enormously refreshing and exciting with endless new possibilities. The resulting artworks are both interpretive and photolike, suspended somewhere between photography and traditional painting. They represent a new art form made possible by a new technology.

Of course the methods of painting from life with a computer can be as varied as that of traditional media. Every artist will approach the challenge of creating a compelling piece of art in a different way, so the descriptions I present represent only some of the possibilities.

This book presents the wide range of styles and subjects that I have explored creating Luminair paintings over the past seven years. It shows many possibilities for artistic experimentation using the Luminair painting technique—rough representations of everyday objects to more sophisticated portrayals of architectural form, atmospheric lighting, graphic stylization, portraits and landscapes.

The book is divided into five chapters. Chapter One provides practical advice to artists regarding Luminair methodology and techniques. Chapters Two, Three and Four present a sampling of my Luminair paintings. Chapter Five shows the work of three guest artists, who continue to break frontiers with this new medium. The paintings in this book were created using both Macintosh and PC Platforms with a variety of imaging software.

Painting in the backyard with an audience of two.

Painting the image on page 81.

My full setup: 15-inch Macintosh G4 PowerBook, Wacom drawing tablet and pen, support board and Anderson water color easel (tripod). The right-side photo shows the easel and vented masonite support board without the computer.

USING A COMPUTER TO PAINT FROM LIFE

The first step I take in a painting is to select a subject or scene of interest. There are many things that intrigue me when considering this, but the most compelling is a dramatic sense of natural light that changes as I create the picture. The changing environment forces a sense of immediacy in my paintings, and usually results in an energetic image that feels alive. I am constantly inspired by nature and surprised by the subtle visual treats that jump out when I look at things closely. The weather and atmospheric conditions also change over time thereby affecting the light; they, too, must be taken into account when considering a given scene.

People often ask me: "Doesn't the glare on your monitor make it difficult or impossible to paint outside?" The answer is: Absolutely! The light pollution on a monitor in full daylight makes it very difficult to see the painting in progress, but there are many ways of coping with this problem. The simplest technique I have found is to wear a black shirt and orient myself so that there is some sort of shadowed or dark area to my back. This will usually take care of the glare. However, direct sunlight may require the use of a hood or shade over the monitor as well. Monitor shades can be bought commercially, but one can be made from black foam board and tape or Velcro. This solution harkens back to the early days of photography, but with Luminair painting the artist's eyes must be constantly moving back and forth between the scene and the painting, so there must be sufficient light to work. I also commonly paint in the back of my minivan; this allows me to be highly mobile but in a nice ambient space where I can see bright natural light without being overwhelmed by it.

Me painting at Union Station.

Laptop computer, Wacom drawing tablet & pen.

Onesimus Nuernberger painting the image on page 127.

Notice the hood on the far laptop to reduce glare.

Ironically, the opposite problem occurs when I try to paint in the dark of night. The monitor's lowest light setting is much brighter than an average dark night. The best way I have found to cope with this is to lay a dark gel or piece of Mylar over the screen to knock down the intensity even lower than what it is designed for. This hack works okay, but the plastic can distort the image and also has an annoying tendency to flop over on the keyboard as I work. A monitor simply does not have the range that human eyes do for seeing clearly in very bright or very dark conditions.

The First Painting:

This is the very first picture I created using the Luminair technique. I made it in late 1999 at a party on my friend's PC using a default paint program whose name I cannot remember. It was produced using a touch pad.

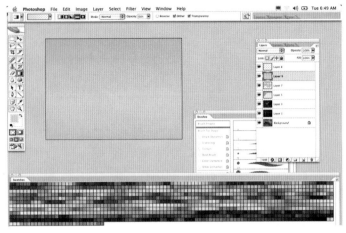

OUTDOOR SCENE PAINTED DURING THE DAY
Establish base color and gradients:

This scene was painted using the laptop set up in the back of my minivan. My first step is usually to fill in the image with the dominant color and value of the scene. Here, the primary colors are blue tones that are prominent in the sky and shadow areas of the scene.

There are seven layers in my file. However, only the top two are for this painting. The other five layers are of different scenes already painted. Making one file with different layers for different paintings allows me to maintain an orderly desktop.

The color palette on the bottom of the screen is a combination of Toyo and Trumatch presets in the Photoshop swatches tool bar. I have expanded the swatches across the bottom of the screen to maximize my viewing area whilst keeping the greatest number of colors showing. I sample from the colors to block in the picture and then, once it is roughed in, I sample from the colors in the picture to detail it out at less than 100% opacity.

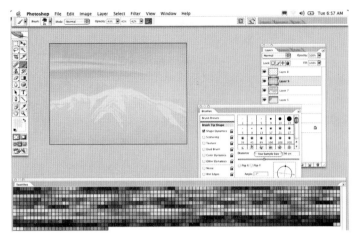

Define the shapes:

The next step in the process is to block in the shapes of the scene with simple color set at 100% opacity. In this case I will not make any sort of line drawing, choosing instead to define the composition with shape and volume.

I am using a simple default round brush. The only modifications I have made are to give it a slightly soft edge and pressure sensitive fall off. Otherwise there are no custom settings or complex tricks used. In this picture the sky and mountains are on one layer and the palm trees in the foreground are on another, each set at 100% opacity. For the paintings in this book I almost always chose a simple setup like this for speed and not to give the image a telltale "digital fingerprint" that identifies it as being created in a specific program at a particular time in its evolution.

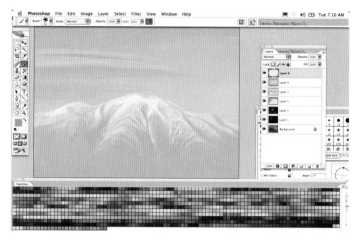

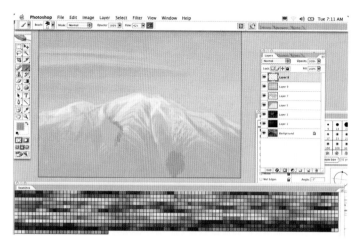

Detail the shapes:

Now I will add some more refined detail to the background elements of the image. Often, for a picture like this one, I will look through binoculars to best capture the minute structures that give naturalistic character to elements too far away for the naked eye to see.

At this point my brush is set at a lower opacity so I can build up subtle gradations and small details without covering up all the work done so far. The blue from the sky that was originally filled in now acts as the shadow areas on the mountain and some tan and pale red show where the rocks are coming through. I have added a more intense blue to the lower section to highlight the intensity of the atmosphere.

Add foreground elements:

The last step in this picture is to create a second layer and paint the palm trees that are in the foreground. First I block them in 100%-opacity base color, then using the layer transparency as a selection, I go back in with a lighter opacity and add detail.

Completed painting:
Mount Baldy, Signal Hill /February 2006
Winter in Southern California

If you are inspired by dramatic and shifting weather patterns, as I am, then Los Angeles is a difficult place to live. The climate here is famous for being "perfect," with perfect defined as constant, moderate temperatures, sunny days, cool nights, and little variation from season to season. This is okay if you like living in a huge, climate-controlled terrarium, but I do not. I go for just the opposite, finding inspiration in nature's raw and changing beauty. There are times that I find Los Angeles rather depressing, as the four seasons here are dry, drier, driest, and wet.

In contrast to the monotony and visual boredom of the long dry season, the rainy season (November through March) is often truly spectacular. Rain washes the dust off the vegetation and buildings, and the air is cleansed of smog and haze. Much to the surprise of many, mountains come into view, rising high above the flat valley floor. This sets up a condition that I have always found fascinating. Snowcapped mountains are a backdrop for a semi-tropical environment where palm trees of many sorts abound. This striking visual scene occurs only when the conditions are just right: on a clear day right after a cool storm has blown through. When such a day comes along, I go out in my minivan seeking views where these elements overlap, and paint them.

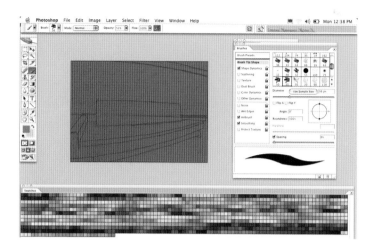

STEP 1

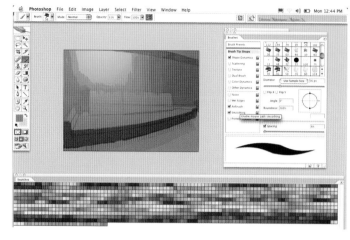

STEP 2

INTERIOR SCENE PAINTED AT NIGHT

Lay out line drawing:

In this image I am going to use a wide-lens effect that approximates the look of a fish-eye or forced-perspective camera. This look has always intrigued me, and I am excited to try it out on a digital life painting. Once I have filled in the layer with a 100%-opacity color, I set the line tool to a darker color at about 40% opacity, and draw some basic perspective outlines and shapes that define the scene. A horizon line starts the layout with some basic vanishing lines curving out toward either side of the picture. Then I rough in the shape of the couch and the elements around it. In order not to make the painting look too technical or stiff, I do not create a full construction of the shapes in proper perspective. Instead, I choose to define just a minimum impression of the space I am going to paint. Subsequently, I fill it in with color and lighting to give a full, if slightly distorted, feeling of the mood of the scene.

Lay in big gradients:

The color I have already chosen to fill in the whole picture is the dominant warm orange wood tone that is pervasive as the base level of the scene. The wood is 50-year old maple paneling, lit with a halogen strip light, so the color is intense and rich. The gradient is a dark version of the orange set to color dodge in the layer options. This creates a strong glow and establishes the primary light direction from above left.

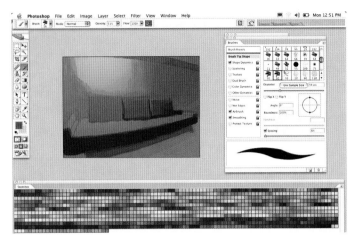

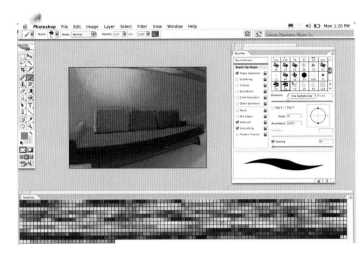

Establish floor and start painting lighting:

Now that the basic scene is established with perspective and some color, I begin adding more definition to the various elements. The floor is white linoleum tile with some sheen to it. For whatever reason this is not showing up from my perspective, so I just put in color and a soft, shadowed area underneath the sofa. Notice how I have included some of the orange wall color in the shadow area under the sofa. This helps unify the scene by connecting the floor with the light source color. I also paint out the perspective construction lines on the sofa cushions. Since at this point the image is just one layer, I simply paint over what is there until I am satisfied with how it looks.

Block in color:

The next step is to block in the color of the main objects in the scene. The couch is a textured red velvet material that really glows in this warm light, so I paint it in with a variety of red hues with the brush set to about 50% opacity on average. I try not to put too many details in at this stage, just define the primary color regions.

I am also starting to add detail to the wood paneling in the form of grain and some softer gradients. Notice the occluded, soft shadow behind the top of the cushions. This effect seems to defy logic, as many visual things in the real world do, but when painted, it looks "just right."

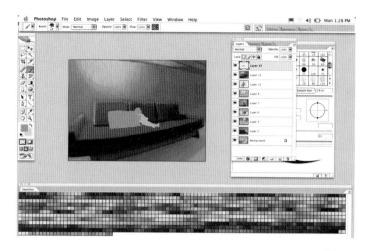

STEP 5

STEP 6

Add foreground elements:

As in the previous exercise, this picture is created as one, 100%-opacity layer in a file that has a few other completed images in it already. Notice the other layers underneath, and try to find the other pictures in this book that they are associated with. As I did in the previous mountain scene, I will now create a new layer for the foreground elements. After the layer is made, I paint in the doll and throw pillow as a 100%-opaque shape.

Shade foreground elements:

I select the foreground elements so when I begin shading them, I can paint right up to the edge without changing their outline and then paint on the new layer with a 50%-opacity brush. I try to sample from the colors already present in the scene, so the new elements properly integrate into the color space of what is there.

15

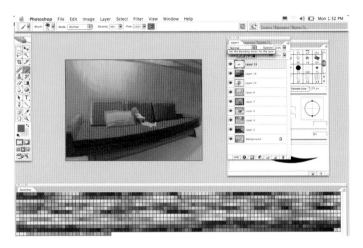

STEP 7

STEP 8

Build gradations on foreground elements:

Now that the basic lighting and color are established on the doll and pillow, I bring in more soft shaded areas and continue to build in the dark areas. Once the shading seems properly balanced, I add in the highlights on the wrinkles of the cushion and the doll. I also notice that I have forgotten some other background elements, like the little end cabinet on the far screen right, so before step 8, I add in these things.

Smooth and add details:

For the first time in the process I will zoom in on the image and evaluate it in terms of detail and texture. Up until now I have been viewing it from afar in order to get the big compositional elements looking good. Zooming in too early can give you a false impression of what is going on in the big picture and is only really needed at the end of the process. With a fairly low-opacity small brush I will sample from the adjacent color of any area and smooth out rough spots, clean up edges and build subtle gradients giving the image a lifelike impression.

Completed painting:

Sarah on Red Couch / April 2006

Wide-angle perspective explores more directions for the Luminair technique.

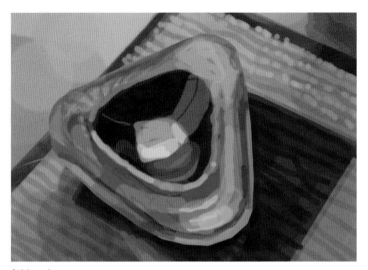

Ashtray / JULY 2001

Big Palm / OCTOBER 2005

LOS ANGELES

I have been living in Los Angeles for twenty years and have a love/hate relation-ship with the place. I have lived in a variety of places around the metro area, from Pasadena to downtown, and most recently in Long Beach. Throughout my residence here, I have periodically tried to escape the brown monotony and ever-increasing congestion of the city. The climate here is so consistently mild for so much of the year that I often feel cut off from nature with her changes and variability. On the flip side, there is no better place to live in the winter when moderate rain and clean wind chase away the haze. While much of the country is stuck in the ice of winter, Angelenos bask in 70-degree temperatures surrounded by clear views of snow-covered mountains.

The paintings in this section give a glimpse of what I see throughout the year liv-ing in this funny place. I am fortunate to live in a beautiful modern house built in

1954 and offering the best conditions for creating pictures on the computer. Generous roof overhangs and mature vegetation create deep shadows with rich pools of light, and it is all framed by a nicely proportioned structure with lots of glass. When I go out, I bring along my computer setup, and sometimes paint in the field. These pictures are often created from the back of my minivan, but occasion-ally I set the easel up in a park or public area.

Ashtray (above left) is the first painting I produced using my Mac G4 PowerBook. It represents the real beginning of the artistic journey documented in this book. I am always fascinated by glass and reflections, so this Christmas gift from a friend was a natural place to start. The picture was done with the touchpad because my tablet was delivered a day later, and I couldn't wait.

Baked Oven / MAY 2006

The *Baked Oven* series breaks free from the use of Luminair painting as just a "snapshot" medium that focuses mostly on lighting and composition. It was a natural fit to combine my love of form and design together with the technique. The result could only be called "photo-cubism!"

Baked Oven 2 /MAY 2006

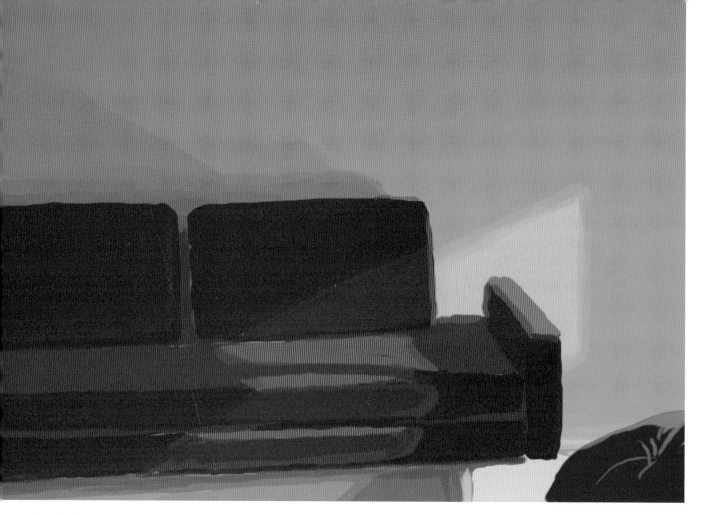

Couch 2 /April 2006

Red velveteen couch in the morning.

The vegetation and lighting in my back yard are ideal subjects for Luminair painting. Rich shadows and pools of light create perfect conditions, and the mature Japanese plantings are diverse and sculptural.

Bamboo /JULY 2001

Tommy /june 2006

This picture was made right after the vet told us our cat would die from kidney failure in a few weeks. I wanted to capture his regal comfort as he slept in his favorite sunny spot. Months have passed since that diagnosis, and Tommy is still enjoying gobs of turkey and drinking copiously from the bathtub faucet with minimal signs of immediate death. Here's to your ninth life big boy!

Brown Bathroom /April 2006

Burling Hall Night Ceiling /May 2006 (next page)

Clock & Walrus / MAY 2006

The chubby walrus is a ceramic made by Arabia in Finland. It was passed down from my grandpa Pugh to my dad and then to me. I have always enjoyed its fat, strong form. It is pictured here with a vintage Sony clock from my brother.

Fun with chrome and glass.

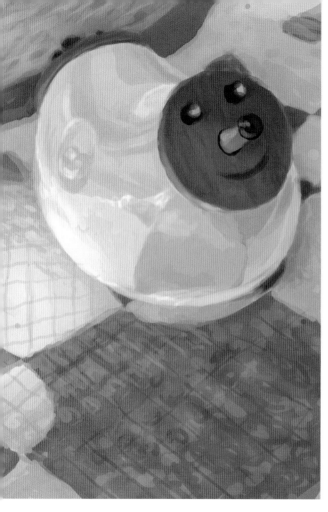

Cookie Jar /AUGUST 2002

A nostalgic piece showing the cookie jar I regularly raided at my Grandma Pugh's house when I was a boy.

Turtle Studies /AUGUST 2002

Turtle Bus is our other cat, a fat female, one-eyed Calico.

Pushing the use of reflections and space. Note: Where am I?

Flower Bathroom /April 2006

Hanging Yucca /MARCH 2006

This yucca decided all on its own to grow horizontally right out in front of our bedroom window. It catches lots of interesting light, especially early in the morning when we are just waking up.

Jacaranda /july 2002

A painting of my friend Paul Kirley's painting. Paul K /may 2002
Thanks, Paul!

Jacaranda: upshot /june 2006

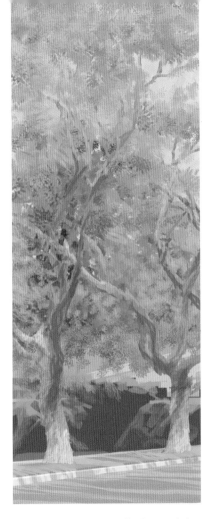

Burling Hall Purple /june 2006

Every June in Los Angeles the Jacaranda trees bloom. Some people swoon over the color, and some complain of the sticky goo given off by the blossoms. I am more of a swooner and have always loved the vibrant purple that envelops our street every season. These paintings give only a hint at the glory of these wonderful trees.

Kitchen /june 2006

A refined study of our kitchen. I think this painting turned out quite well, capturing sublime architectural details with subtle lighting and gradations.

LB Yard 1 & 2 /AUGUST 2002   The lighting at night in our garden is ideal for the Luminair technique. The value and saturation of what is seen are very close to what is displayed on the monitor, so the usual conflicts that are evident in bright day shots are no longer problematic.

LB Yard 5 /july 2002

Yard 3 /august 2001

Mirror /september 2001   Another reflection study.

Munktiki /march 2006   Inspired by my brother-in-law's interest in all things tiki, this painting shows Evil Bastard arbitrating a debt between two friends in the foreground.

Rainy Backyard /February 2005

Roofline /FEBRUARY 2002   Experimenting with using only the Photoshop "line tool" for a whole painting.

Randy /APRIL 2003   These portraits show some exploration in applying the technique to figurative paint-ing, including this one of my brother-in-law.

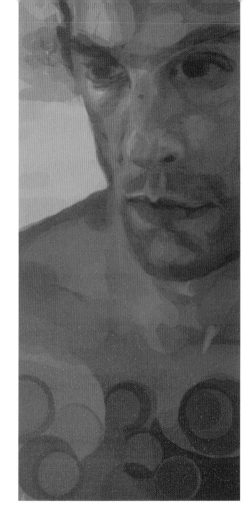

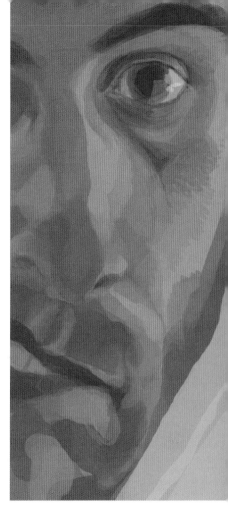

Self-Portrait Series /MAY 2002

Red Moon /october 2002

Speed /february 2002   A maximum-speed painting of an aircraft banking
over the tree in our yard.

A classic Los Angeles sunset with wires and all, from our side yard.

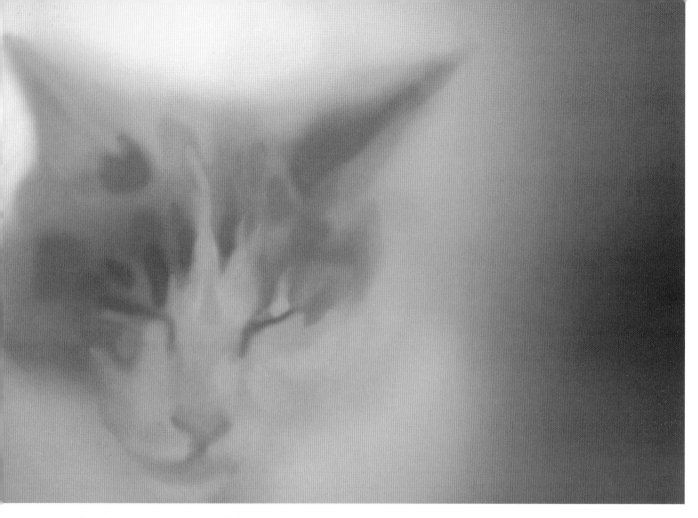

Sleeping Turtle Bus /April 2005

Turtle Bus sleeps a lot, too, and it is fun to watch her as she lounges in "her" chair. Here I am experimenting with a big, soft blur technique that vignettes the surrounding scene and forms the focal point.

Soft Silky Boat /APRIL 2005

Side Yard 6 / JULY 2001

Vertical 1 / MAY 2006

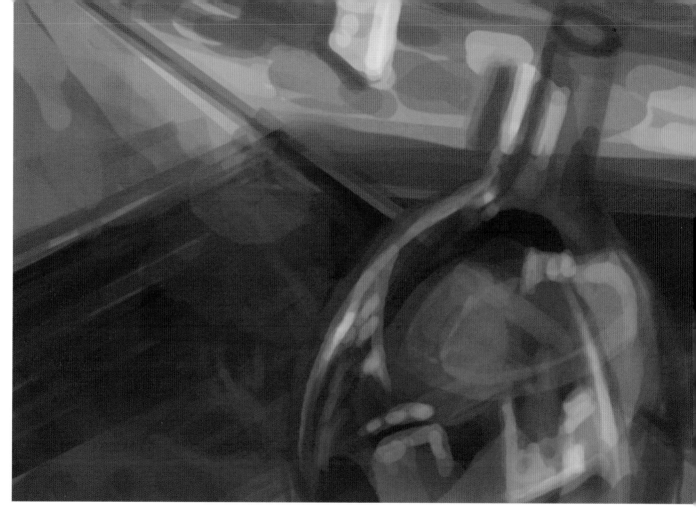

An early material study.

(next page) In this tighter painting, I wanted to capture the grandeur of the original Crane sink and Formica counter in our guest bathroom.

Blue Bottle /august 2001

Wide Sink /may 2006 (next page)

Stump / AUGUST 2001

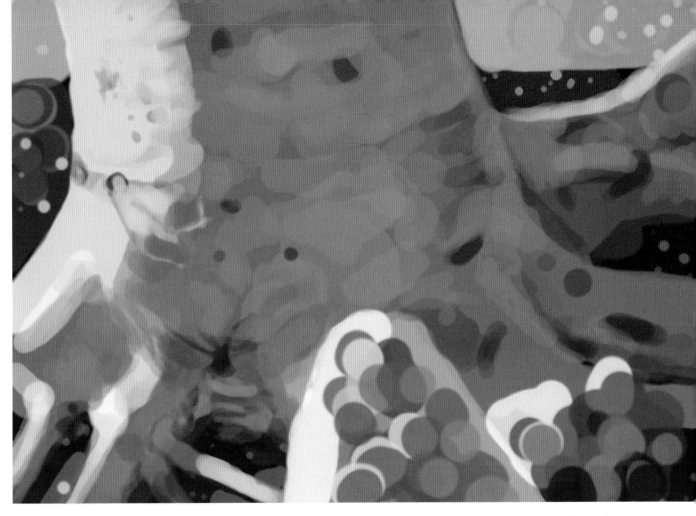

Stump 2 /August 2001

Sonja Orchids /April 2006

These orchids from our house were painted for my mother-in-law's birthday.
Her father grew orchids and this variety is one of her favorites.

Spring Roses /MAY 2006

Hot Palm /october 2005

Palm Sunset Series /november 2005
(right page)

On Wednesday, November 16, 2005, the first big Santa Ana wind of the season blew in over Long Beach. As the sun fell in the western sky, it bathed the palm trees to the east of my studio in a shimmering, golden light. It was about 4:00 p.m. I went outside in the parking lot, set up my laptop computer on its easel, opened Photoshop, and began to paint the scene.

The wind blew clean across the palm fronds as I worked to capture the light and energy of the ebbing day and setting sun. By the time I began the second painting 45 minutes later, the full moon started to rise above the dilapidated rooftops of the industrial buildings across the alley from my shop. What a fantastic sight. I rapidly threw down 100%-opacity color trying to capture the shifting orb as it passed to the left of the tree, up, and out of frame.

Finally, as the sun reached its most rich orange hue, I moved to the next set of trees, just to the right, and painted it as the light changed to a muted, warm grey and then on into dusk.

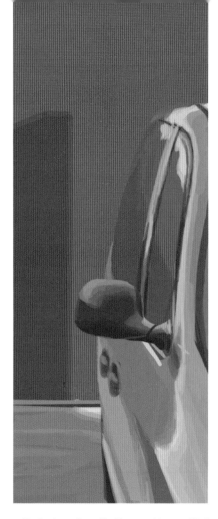

Minivan Series /november 2005

My fondness for reflections continues with these studies of my glorious 1997 Plymouth Voyager minivan.

A very quick painting done outside my studio door just after a winter rainstorm.

Rain Chair /DECEMBER 2005

Storm Sunset 2 / january 2006

A couple of cloud studies painted as a storm passed outside my studio and over the sunset.

Storm Sunset 3 /january 2006

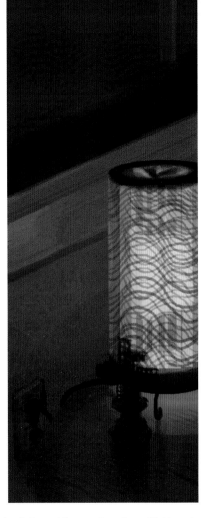

Zooming in toward the moon's surface with binoculars allows me to capture more detail than with the naked eye.

The east view with the inevitable monthly rise of the full moon rise is always a great inspiration.
The moon is a perfect subject; it moves and changes, but not too fast.

Sunwedge Dusk Dark / july 2002

Night in Long Beach / july 2002

California Street /january 2006

This picture is the only one in this book that was produced for a client. A friend of mine is a real estate agent and wanted to experiment with some gift ideas for his buyers, so we printed this picture of their new house as an address card for them to send out to friends and family.

Church Alley /MARCH 2006

Francis & Ellie /FEBRUARY 2002   This is a painting of Francis and Eleanor Coppola relaxing at their winery. They are very kind and generous people. I captured this view during a brainstorming symposium for a few designer colleagues and myself held at their home.

This was painted on a camping trip to Joshua Tree Park. My friends and I were sitting around the campfire watching it burn. The moving flames and ever-changing log pile presented an interesting challenge.

Fire 3 /october 2003

Palm Snow, Signal Hill /February 2006

Palm Snow On Huntington Drive /March 2006

Whitley Heights /SEPTEMBER 2001

These pictures were painted in the days following 9/11 when my brother, Dave, was planning his move from Hollywood Heights to Manhattan. They exude a quiet sadness and the pensive feelings I had at the time together with the pride I have for my brother's career advancement and the fear of his moving to New York.

Here is my brother as we talked about the events unfolding at the time.

Shoot /MARCH 2002

These paintings were created during a photo shoot for a Nissan project I was working on. I had all my equipment, and the lighting was so interesting that I just had to paint it.

South Pasadena Park /February 2006

South Pasadena /February 2006

Westchester Wide /February 2006 (next page)

(next page) A panorama of the clear winter view from the hilltop in Westchester, California.

Snow Palms From Pasadena City College /February 2006

I painted this series during an outing to Union Station in downtown Los Angeles. Artist Robh Ruppel teaches a class in Digital Landscape at Art Center, and he allowed me to tag along on this particular excursion. It was exciting to see all his students using their laptops as painting tools. The varied results show the great promise of this technique.

Union Station Series /march 2006

Hitch /AUGUST 2003

Mom's Corner /OCTOBER 2003

Throughout my life, I have spent part of each year on the East Coast with my family. When I was a child, we usually spent three months there in the summer, and, if we were lucky, another few weeks over the winter holidays. Now, as an adult, I feel fortunate to still have some flexibility in my schedule. In spite of professional demands, I usually make it back East for at least a few weeks each year. My visits are spent vacationing with family or working on projects, and they are always a time of artistic growth for me. Swimming, hiking in the woods, and living in a rural setting provide a great re-set away from urban life, and my time there always gives me a fresh perspective.

This section highlights Luminair paintings completed during this wonderful time of renewal. My subjects are often related to nature, and include woodsy settings, water scenes, local architecture, and the dramatic, ever-changing weather. My primary locations are the family farm in Gilmanton, New Hampshire, my grandma's longtime home in Needham, Massachusetts, and the area around my brother and sister-in-law's apartment in New York City.

NEW ENGLAND & NEW YORK

The summer of 2003 was one of the best in my life. I was in New England surrounded by family and friends. Everyone was there, and we shared many happy family events. Best of all, I was with my wife and new baby daughter, Serena. We all had a great time. My mom was a new grandma, and she was very happy. Then a week after we got back to Long Beach, I learned that she was seriously ill with melanoma, and her prognosis didn't look great. A sadness broke the afterglow of that lovely summer. We went back to New Hampshire again for her surgery and to help take care of her.

The fall was spectacular with cool nights, warm days, and a good mix of sun and rain. The countryside was beautiful and colorful, but my feelings were apprehensive. I wanted to capture the beauty of the setting, but inside I feared the worst, and the artwork reflects this split.

Mower / july 2003

I love funny vehicles—what can I say?

Cape Cod 1 / july 2003

The Pugh family has been going to Cape Cod in the summers for as long as I can remember, usually near Chatham. Since my childhood, it has always been a pleasure to stay with them. I now return to these familiar scenes with my own family. During this particular summer, we all stayed together at a fabulous place: a spacious house standing on a bluff about seventy feet above the water. To the east there was an unobstructed view of the harbor and the grand bay formed by inlets from the ocean. It spread out before us spanning a full 180 degrees. The Eastern exposure has always been my favorite. I love the sunrise and then, later in the evening, seeing the moonrise on the same scene. My grandma was 85 that year, and it was special to share the summer with her and my wife and our new baby daughter. My Aunt Abbi, also an artist, had her canvas and paints set up on the bluff, and the whole atmosphere was very inspiring.

On yet another splendid day, I was once again facing east, entranced by the changing light and the brilliance of the newly rising sun. Sunrise is always an exciting time for me to work, so I got up early and set up my easel on this cool summer morning. The quality of the water and the light and the color of the boats was at first very comfortable to paint. But then, as the sun slowly began to rise, it became more difficult to interpret the colors. Right at this moment, there was a bright intensity from the sun that I couldn't capture on my monitor. It was a deep magenta too difficult to reproduce. Once the sun was up, I was able to capture the highly-saturated colors and the fiery quality of the landscape as the sun hit the water and boat. I worked for about two hours on these four paintings.

Cape Cod 3 / july 2003

Cape Cod 4 /july 2003

Cape Cod 5 / july 2003

This sailboat shows how pristine the water and colors were. My brother, Dave, and Aunt Abbi were trolling around in the boat, and I was able to capture the image quickly before they moved on.

I painted this picture using binoculars. I love the idea of zooming in on a distant scene like a photographer, and was excited about using this technique. First I roughed in the larger image, and then I got the detail using the binoculars.

Cape Cod 6 /july 2003

Neil /AUGUST 2006

During my childhood summers in New England, I would watch my Uncle Neil and his band play rock-and-roll every Sunday night. He has been practicing since before I can remember with the three or four other guys in the band. In the space below his two-car garage, he built a state-of-the-art recording studio where they can play without disturbing Grandma, who sleeps upstairs.

Neil's son, Chris Canney, also has a band and practices in the same space. On two different nights, I sat in on their rehearsals and painted both father and son. Without photo reference, it is hard to find a situation where one can paint a candid portrait. Subjects must stay relatively still and involved in an activity that holds their attention. In this case, playing music was perfect.

Chris /august 2006

Chaffies /AUGUST 2003

Loon Pond in the Moonlight /AUGUST 2003
(right page)

For as long as I can remember, I have spent summers at my Grammy's farm near Loon Pond in Gilmanton, New Hampshire. When I painted these pictures, we were staying at a cabin right next to the pond. Painting this view of the moon was exciting. The challenges were different from those I faced when working in the bright sun. When I work in full sunlight, the monitor isn't bright enough to show me the scene. But just the opposite is true on a moonlit night, when the monitor is incredibly bright, way more than the natural light at that time. It is difficult to adjust my eyes from the dim moonlight to the bright monitor, so I often need to squint.

I took my easel onto the dock and watched the fishing boats tied up there. It was midnight and unusually hot with mosquitoes buzzing around. As is so often the case, I had to work quickly. The composition kept changing as the moon's reflection edged alongside the dock towards where I was standing. When I was done, I took a dip into the water. Afterwards, I felt great.

Needham, Massachusetts /DECEMBER 2001

Abbi's Big Tomato /AUGUST 2003
{right page}

Long before heirloom tomatoes became popular, my mother and Aunt Abbi were growing fabulous, "old" red tomatoes. They were wonderful to look at and wonderful to eat. I wanted to capture their juiciness; the way the light glowed inside them, and especially the bumps and wrinkles that made them supermarket rejects. One day, I was sitting in the sun on my grandma's porch eating a Cherokee purple tomato, my favorite kind. It is more deeply red and wrinkled than other varieties, a little funny looking and not perfectly round. But the earth it is grown in, the humidity of the summers, and my aunt's loving care make it the best-tasting tomato ever.

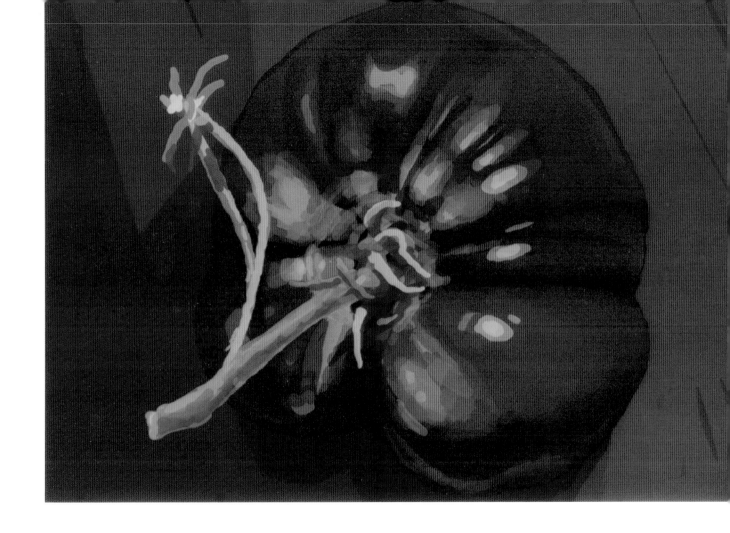

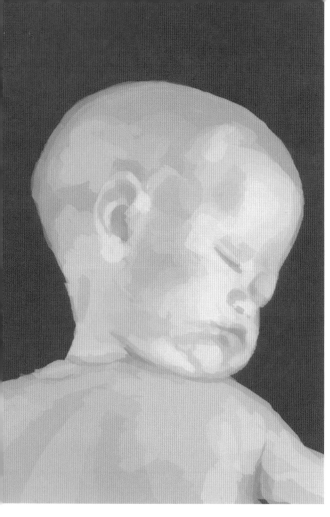

Serena /AUGUST 2003   My daughter, Serena, sleeping while I painted the pond surface.

Barn Window /JULY 2003

It's late in the afternoon. Today is hot and humid, and people are swimming on the beach. The light is fantastic. Bright rays pierce through the water and hit the sand below. The shadows and light play on the water. People are having fun and finding relief from the heat. Shortly after, there's a big thunderstorm, but I've already caught this pleasant and familiar scene.

Loon Pond / AUGUST 2003

Loon 1 & 2 /AUGUST 2003   It's early in the morning, and I am looking out the window of our cabin on Loon Pond. Eileen and Serena are sleeping. Serena is just a baby, only four months old. I can see the water through a curtain of lacy green leaves. The sun is just beginning to rise, and the water shimmers with reflections in the early morning light. I'm fascinated by the ever-changing quality of the water's surface.

How can I work quickly enough to capture the ripples from a fish's nose penetrating the waters surface?

Loon 3 & 4 /august 2003

Up Leaves /october 2003

Winter Flowers /december 2005

A view of my Grandmother's sink facing north over the cold New Hampshire winterscape.

Winter Sink /december 2001

Winter Trees /january 2006

Red Shed Window / AUGUST 2003

I'm looking west across my grandmother's hayfield toward our neighbor's house and the mountains beyond. It's a classic New Hampshire scene and one painted by generations of our family: the broad, golden field, glimmering pond, and bright flowers, all edged by old fences, trees, and stone walls, with the old farmhouse in the distance.

Car /AUGUST 2003

A winter shot of my mom's car as we were stressfully getting ready to depart.

About To Leave /DECEMBER 2005

My Loves /AUGUST 2005

I am the luckiest man. These are two of the loveliest ladies in my life: my wife Eileen and daughter Serena (the third is my mom). This painting depicts Eileen's birthday on the farm in Gilmanton. Serena is getting ready to help blow out the candles and dig in to the melting ice cream cake. The arm of Serena's great-gram, Laurose, appears in the upper right of the picture. Unlike almost all the pictures in this book, this one is partially painted with photo reference. It was just too difficult to get my little girl to sit there and watch the ice cream cake melt while her dad slaved away on his computer!

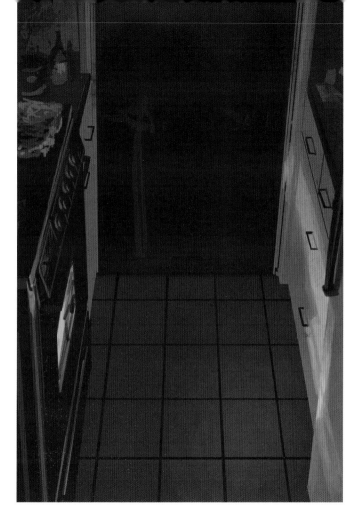

This picture captures the small space my brother, Dave, shared with his then-fiancée, Tina.

Manhattan Apartment /DECEMBER 2001

A view of our gate at the airport before we boarded. The heavy snow made us nervous, but we had a spectacular flight home.

Gate 4 /JANUARY 2006

W Hotel /december 2001

W Hotel 2 /december 2001

A different view from Dave and Tina's Gramercy apartment.

New York /DECEMBER 2001

79th & 3rd /DECEMBER 2005

Amsterdam /november 2003

Rio 1 /april 2005

Rio 3 /april 2005

Using a laptop as a painting tool has great benefits. One that I especially like is the ability to create art easily when on a trip. The light weight and compact power of the digital medium allows artists to carry a full studio right along with them, even in adverse conditions. I have explored the potential of being an "itinerant" artist to some degree, but fantasize completing more exotic and demanding trips with my "studio" at my side.

This section shows the paintings I did during recent travels to Europe, South America, and Hawaii. I hope these works inspire other artists to continue pushing the limits of this new technology even further.

Amsterdam (above left) is a view from my hotel room in Amsterdam. I wanted the colors and slight distortion to reflect the strange altered state of this place.

The crude paintings in the *Rio* series (above center and right) were captured on our latest trip to South America. I was hesitant to bring my laptop computer because of its size and the fact that it was the first big trip with our two-year-old daughter. So I resorted to using my stepmother's PC to paint these images of Rio de Janeiro from our apartment. They were created using the touch pad...ouch.

Car Flip /december 2003   As I was stopped on the side of the road painting these funny tall pine trees, a blue Peugeot went sliding past my left side and flipped end-over-end, eventually coming to rest on its side in a ditch. I was literally able to catch the gesture of the car crashing as it happened. I did, however, jump out quickly to check on the person inside (who was okay).

Another painting from the *Car Flip* series.

Tall Trees /december 2003

Essen /november 2003   A view from my hotel room in Germany.

Loire Castle /november 2003   The castle in Saumur.

The first view of my favorite city on the trip, Saumur.

Loire View /NOVEMBER 2003

Loire Road /NOVEMBER 2003

Loire Trees /NOVEMBER 2003

Fall colors in the Loire.

Saumur riverfront.

Crystal Hotel /november 2003

The view from my hotel room in Saumur, France.

Images painted in the tradition of impressionists like Monet of the water's surface as it roils.

Loire Water /NOVEMBER 2003

Rio 2 /April 2005

Serena In Forest /March 2005

A quick sketch of my daughter tramping along a trail in Kauai.

Here is an early morning view of the beach at the Mauna Kea resort where we had a splendid stay for our friend's wedding.

Hawaii /OCTOBER 2003

One of the most exciting times in the evolution of any new art form occurs at the experimental stage. A new generation of artists emerges and begins to experiment and define a wide variety of styles and personal looks. Luminair painting is at that point right now. There are many artists who are practicing this method and trying out new approaches and techniques. I was not able to include more than a few in this book. The following are three of my favorites.

Robh Ruppel, who teaches a new course at Art Center College of Design that uses this technique for quick sketching in the field, has produced some fantastic works of his own around the Los Angeles area. His work shows the great promise for digital plein air painting to give a comparable emotional impact to traditional mediums such as oil, acrylic, or watercolor and his skill with these classic mediums can be seen in his digital art with its subtle use of lighting and color.

Nicolas Bouvier (also known as Sparth) is a fantastic and talented French artist who has been doing some wonderful experiments with the technique for the past few years. He is one of the world's leading concept artists for video games and his keen design sense and advanced use of Photoshop has resulted in some of the best work so far. Onesimus Neurenberger's piece represents the fine student work that is being produced, and is an example of what we can expect from the future as more and more people begin to take their notebook computers out in the field and capture the wonders of the world they see. The artists speak for themselves in this chapter.

Robh Ruppel (*opposite page*):
The painting to the left was done as a demo for my Digital Landscape class that I teach at Art Center. We were painting in the parking lot of the Rose Bowl that day. I thought the values worked out nicely, but it looks a little strange that the tree is growing out of the pavement, which it really is doing by the way.

June 2 /ROBH RUPPEL   You wouldn't know it to look at the picture, but this was one of the hottest days of the year. We were situated under a lot of oak trees in Eaton Canyon just past the stream. The temperature was nice and there was a slight breeze. I realized how hot it really was when I got back to my car! Nature was nicer than the asphalt frying pan cooking my automobile. This was done in Painter 9.

This is a painting I did while in the Digital Landscape Painting class at Art Center. Nick came to paint with us that day at Los Angeles Union Station. He sat to one side with his wife, just outside the bagel shop, which I thought made for an interesting composition. I also liked the mix of different textures and surfaces in the walls and floor.

I started the painting by blocking in large, flat shapes of color. Then I created tile grids and pasted them into perspective on the walls and floor. Next I painted in reflections above and below the grid layers. Refining my shapes, adding hue variations, and blending were next. Finally, I added small highlights along tile edges, and painted random strokes to create the wall textures.

Nick Pugh at LA Union Station /onesimus nuernberger

With Nick's process in mind, I tested these digital painting techniques in 2005. With a friend, I walked around Montreal (where I was living at the time), painting vignettes with no other rule than spontaneity. This painting was done in downtown Montreal while having a drink in a café.

Whenever I go back to France, I enjoy spending a few days in the Chateau de Montaclier. For generations, the family of my wife Lorene has lived on this large property in the middle of Auvergne, very close to the volcano chain. The castle itself was built mainly in the 19th century, although the foundations are much older. This is a view from the eastern stairs, behind a small fountain representing a sea creature. Many parts of the metal structure are missing, but that adds a lot to the charm of the place.

127

other titles by design studio press:

Lift Off:
air vehicle sketches & renderings
from the drawthrough collection
ISBN-13: 978-1-933492-15-5

Start Your Engines:
surface vehicle sketches & renderings
from the drawthrough collection
ISBN-13: 978-1-933492-13-1

Concept Design 2
ISBN 10: 1-9334-9202-3

Daphne 01: the art of daphne yap
ISBN 10: 1-933492-09-0

The Skillful Huntsman
ISBN 10: 0-9726-6764-4

LA/SF: a sketchbook from california
ISBN 10: 1-9334-9210-4

Doodles: 200 5-minute doodles
ISBN-13: 978-1-933492-22-3

Worlds: a mission of discovery
ISBN 10: 0-9726-6769-5

AVP: the creature effects of ADI
ISBN 10: 0-9726-6765-2

The Art of Darkwatch
ISBN 10: 1-9334-9201-5

Monstruo: the art of carlos huante
ISBN 10: 0-9726-6762-8

Mas Creaturas:
monstruo addendum
ISBN 10: 1-9334-9207-4

Quantum Dreams:
the art of stephan martinière
ISBN 10: 0-9726-6767-9

Quantumscapes:
the art of stephan martinière
ISBN-13: 978-1-933492-51-3

Entropia:
a collection of unusually rare stamps
ISBN 10: 1-933492-04-X

2 DAY LOAN

776 PUG.

Guest Artist Contact Info:

www.robhruppel.com
www.onesimusnuernberger.com
www.sparth.com

To order additional copies of this book and
to view other books we offer, please visit:
www.designstudiopress.com

For volume purchases and resale
inquiries please e-mail:
info@designstudiopress.com

Or you can write to:
Design Studio Press
8577 Higuera Street
Culver City, CA 90232
tel 310.836.3116
fax 310.836.1136

ABOUT THE AUTHOR

Nick Pugh has had a passion for creativity and art his entire life.
Over the past seven years, he has been experimenting with a new
art form: Luminair painting. In addition to painting, Nick teaches
Originality at Art Center College of Design. For the past ten years,
he has been a lead concept artist for the visual effects studio
Rhythm & Hues. Recent film projects include *The Chronicles of
Narnia*, *Fast and Furious 3*, *Serenity*, and *Superman Returns*. He
also creates unique personal concept cars and vehicular sculptures.
His work has appeared in numerous publications and television
shows. He holds a B.S. in transportation design from Art Center.
Nick lives with his wife and daughter in Long Beach, California.

Instructional DVDs by **design studio press**
and **the gnomon workshop:**
Authored by **Nick Pugh**

Originality in Design:
Creating a Unique Form Language

Creature Design Illustration:
Form Language Refinement

Creature & Environment Rendering
Digital Rendering Techniques

To order these DVDs and to view other
DVDs we offer, please visit:
www.thegnomonworkshop.com

421903